Rivers to the Sea

Rivers to the Sea
Sara Teasdale

MINT EDITIONS

Rivers to the Sea was first published in 1915.

This edition published by Mint Editions 2021.

ISBN 9781513295954 | E-ISBN 9781513297453

Published by Mint Editions®

 MINT
EDITIONS
minteditionbooks.com

Publishing Director: Jennifer Newens
Design & Production: Rachel Lopez Metzger
Project Manager: Micaela Clark
Typesetting: Westchester Publishing Services

Contents

Part V

Sappho

PART I

SPRING NIGHT

The park is filled with night and fog,
    The veils are drawn about the world,
The drowsy lights along the paths
    Are dim and pearled.

Gold and gleaming the empty streets,
    Gold and gleaming the misty lake,
The mirrored lights like sunken swords,
    Glimmer and shake.

Oh, is it not enough to be
Here with this beauty over me?
My throat should ache with praise, and I
Should kneel in joy beneath the sky.
Oh, beauty are you not enough?

Why am I crying after love
With youth, a singing voice and eyes
To take earth's wonder with surprise?
Why have I put off my pride,
Why am I unsatisfied,
I for whom the pensive night
Binds her cloudy hair with light,
I for whom all beauty burns
Like incense in a million urns?
Oh, beauty, are you not enough?
Why am I crying after love?

The Flight

Look back with longing eyes and know that I will follow,
Lift me up in your love as a light wind lifts a swallow,
Let our flight be far in sun or windy rain—
But What If I Heard My First Love Calling Me Again?

Hold me on your heart as the brave sea holds the foam,
Take me far away to the hills that hide your home;
Peace shall thatch the roof and love shall latch the door—
But What If I Heard My First Love Calling Me Once More?

NEW LOVE AND OLD

In my heart the old love
    Struggled with the new;
It was ghostly waking
    All night thru.

Dear things, kind things,
    That my old love said,
Ranged themselves reproachfully
    Round my bed.

But I could not heed them,
    For I seemed to see
The eyes of my new love
    Fixed on me.

Old love, old love,
    How can I be true?
Shall I be faithless to myself
    Or to you?

The Look

Strephon kissed me in the spring,
   Robin in the fall,
But Colin only looked at me
   And never kissed at all.

Strephon's kiss was lost in jest,
   Robin's lost in play,
But the kiss in Colin's eyes
   Haunts me night and day.

SPRING

In Central Park the lovers sit,
    On every hilly path they stroll,
Each thinks his love is infinite,
    And crowns his soul.

But we are cynical and wise,
    We walk a careful foot apart,
You make a little joke that tries
    To hide your heart.

Give over, we have laughed enough;
    Oh dearest and most foolish friend,
Why do you wage a war with love
    To lose your battle in the end?

THE LIGHTED WINDOW

He said:

"In the winter dusk
When the pavements were gleaming with rain,
I walked thru a dingy street
Hurried, harassed,
Thinking of all my problems that never are solved.
Suddenly out of the mist, a flaring gas-jet
Shone from a huddled shop.
I saw thru the bleary window
A mass of playthings:
False-faces hung on strings,
Valentines, paper and tinsel,
Tops of scarlet and green,
Candy, marbles, jacks—
A confusion of color
Pathetically gaudy and cheap.
All of my boyhood
Rushed back.
Once more these things were treasures
Wildly desired.
With covetous eyes I looked again at the marbles,
The precious agates, the pee-wees, the chinies—
Then I passed on.

In the winter dusk,
The pavements were gleaming with rain;
There in the lighted window
I left my boyhood."

The Kiss

Before you kissed me only winds of heaven
    Had kissed me, and the tenderness of rain—
Now you have come, how can I care for kisses
      Like theirs again?

I sought the sea, she sent her winds to meet me,
    They surged about me singing of the south—
I turned my head away to keep still holy
      Your kiss upon my mouth.

And swift sweet rains of shining April weather
    Found not my lips where living kisses are;
I bowed my head lest they put out my glory
      As rain puts out a star.

I am my love's and he is mine forever,
    Sealed with a seal and safe forevermore—
Think you that I could let a beggar enter
      Where a king stood before?

Swans

Night is over the park, and a few brave stars
    Look on the lights that link it with chains of gold,
The lake bears up their reflection in broken bars
    That seem too heavy for tremulous water to hold.

We watch the swans that sleep in a shadowy place,
    And now and again one wakes and uplifts its head;
How still you are—your gaze is on my face—
    We watch the swans and never a word is said.

The Old Maid

I saw her in a Broadway car,
    The woman I might grow to be;
I felt my lover look at her
    And then turn suddenly to me.

Her hair was dull and drew no light
    And yet its color was as mine;
Her eyes were strangely like my eyes
    Tho' love had never made them shine.

Her body was a thing grown thin,
    Hungry for love that never came;
Her soul was frozen in the dark
    Unwarmed forever by love's flame.

I felt my lover look at her
    And then turn suddenly to me,—
His eyes were magic to defy
    The woman I shall never be.

FROM THE WOOLWORTH TOWER

Vivid with love, eager for greater beauty
Out of the night we come
Into the corridor, brilliant and warm.
A metal door slides open,
And the lift receives us.
Swiftly, with sharp unswerving flight
The car shoots upward,
And the air, swirling and angry,
Howls like a hundred devils.
Past the maze of trim bronze doors,
Steadily we ascend.
I cling to you
Conscious of the chasm under us,
And a terrible whirring deafens my ears.

The flight is ended.

We pass thru a door leading onto the ledge—
Wind, night and space
Oh terrible height
Why have we sought you?
Oh bitter wind with icy invisible wings
Why do you beat us?
Why would you bear us away?
We look thru the miles of air,
The cold blue miles between us and the city,
Over the edge of eternity we look
On all the lights,
A thousand times more numerous than the stars;
Oh lines and loops of light in unwound chains
That mark for miles and miles
The vast black mazy cobweb of the streets;
Near us clusters and splashes of living gold
That change far off to bluish steel
Where the fragile lights on the Jersey shore

Tremble like drops of wind-stirred dew.
The strident noises of the city
Floating up to us
Are hallowed into whispers.
Ferries cross thru the darkness
Weaving a golden thread into the night,
Their whistles weird shadows of sound.

We feel the millions of humanity beneath us,—
The warm millions, moving under the roofs,
Consumed by their own desires;
Preparing food,
Sobbing alone in a garret,
With burning eyes bending over a needle,
Aimlessly reading the evening paper,
Dancing in the naked light of the café,
Laying out the dead,
Bringing a child to birth—
The sorrow, the torpor, the bitterness, the frail joy
Come up to us
Like a cold fog wrapping us round.
Oh in a hundred years
Not one of these blood-warm bodies
But will be worthless as clay.
The anguish, the torpor, the toil
Will have passed to other millions
Consumed by the same desires.
Ages will come and go,
Darkness will blot the lights
And the tower will be laid on the earth.
The sea will remain
Black and unchanging,
The stars will look down
Brilliant and unconcerned.

Beloved,
Tho' sorrow, futility, defeat
Surround us,

They cannot bear us down.
Here on the abyss of eternity
Love has crowned us
For a moment
Victors.

At Night

We are apart; the city grows quiet between us,
    She hushes herself, for midnight makes heavy her eyes,
The tangle of traffic is ended, the cars are empty,
    Five streets divide us, and on them the moonlight lies.

Oh are you asleep, or lying awake, my lover?
    Open your dreams to my love and your heart to my words,
I send you my thoughts—the air between us is laden,
    My thoughts fly in at your window, a flock of wild birds.

THE YEARS

Tonight I close my eyes and see
A strange procession passing me—
The years before I saw your face
Go by me with a wistful grace;
They pass, the sensitive shy years,
As one who strives to dance, half blind with tears.

The years went by and never knew
That each one brought me nearer you;
Their path was narrow and apart
And yet it led me to your heart—
Oh sensitive shy years, oh lonely years,
That strove to sing with voices drowned in tears.

Peace

Peace flows into me
    As the tide to the pool by the shore;
    It is mine forevermore,
It ebbs not back like the sea.

I am the pool of blue
    That worships the vivid sky;
    My hopes were heaven-high,
They are all fulfilled in you.

I am the pool of gold
    When sunset burns and dies,—
    You are my deepening skies,
Give me your stars to hold.

April

The roofs are shining from the rain,
    The sparrows twitter as they fly,
And with a windy April grace
    The little clouds go by.

Yet the back-yards are bare and brown
    With only one unchanging tree—
I could not be so sure of Spring
    Save that it sings in me.

SARA TEASDALE

Come

Come, when the pale moon like a petal
    Floats in the pearly dusk of spring,
Come with arms outstretched to take me,
    Come with lips pursed up to cling.

Come, for life is a frail moth flying
    Caught in the web of the years that pass,
And soon we two, so warm and eager
    Will be as the gray stones in the grass.

Moods

I am the still rain falling,
    Too tired for singing mirth—
Oh, be the green fields calling,
    Oh, be for me the earth!

I am the brown bird pining
    To leave the nest and fly—
Oh, be the fresh cloud shining,
    Oh, be for me the sky!

April Song

Willow in your April gown
    Delicate and gleaming,
Do you mind in years gone by
    All my dreaming?

Spring was like a call to me
    That I could not answer,
I was chained to loneliness,
    I, the dancer.

Willow, twinkling in the sun,
    Still your leaves and hear me,
I can answer spring at last,
    Love is near me!

MAY DAY

The shining line of motors,
    The swaying motor-bus,
The prancing dancing horses
    Are passing by for us.

The sunlight on the steeple,
    The toys we stop to see,
The smiling passing people
    Are all for you and me.

"I love you and I love you!"—
    "And oh, I love you, too!"—
"All of the flower girl's lilies
    Were only grown for you!"

Fifth Avenue and April
    And love and lack of care—
The world is mad with music
    Too beautiful to bear.

CROWNED

I wear a crown invisible and clear,
    And go my lifted royal way apart
    Since you have crowned me softly in your heart
With love that is half ardent, half austere;
And as a queen disguised might pass anear
    The bitter crowd that barters in a mart,
    Veiling her pride while tears of pity start,
I hide my glory thru a jealous fear.
My crown shall stay a sweet and secret thing
    Kept pure with prayer at evensong and morn,
    And when you come to take it from my head,
    I shall not weep, nor will a word be said,
But I shall kneel before you, oh my king,
    And bind my brow forever with a thorn.

To a Castilian Song

We held the book together timidly,
    Whose antique music in an alien tongue
    Once rose among the dew-drenched vines that hung
Beneath a high Castilian balcony.
I felt the lute strings' ancient ecstasy,
    And while he read, my love-filled heart was stung,
    And throbbed, as where an ardent bird has clung
The branches tremble on a blossomed tree.
Oh lady for whose sake the song was made,
Laid long ago in some still cypress shade,
    Divided from the man who longed for thee,
        Here in a land whose name he never heard,
        His song brought love as April brings the bird,
    And not a breath divides my love from me!

Broadway

This is the quiet hour; the theaters
    Have gathered in their crowds, and steadily
    The million lights blaze on for few to see,
Robbing the sky of stars that should be hers.
A woman waits with bag and shabby furs,
    A somber man drifts by, and only we
    Pass up the street unwearied, warm and free,
For over us the olden magic stirs.
Beneath the liquid splendor of the lights
    We live a little ere the charm is spent;
This night is ours, of all the golden nights,
        The pavement an enchanted palace floor,
      And Youth the player on the viol, who sent
        A strain of music thru an open door.

A Winter Bluejay

Crisply the bright snow whispered,
Crunching beneath our feet;
Behind us as we walked along the parkway,
Our shadows danced,
Fantastic shapes in vivid blue.
Across the lake the skaters
Flew to and fro,
With sharp turns weaving
A frail invisible net.
In ecstasy the earth
Drank the silver sunlight;
In ecstasy the skaters
Drank the wine of speed;
In ecstasy we laughed
Drinking the wine of love.
Had not the music of our joy
Sounded its highest note?
But no,
For suddenly, with lifted eyes you said,
"Oh look!"
There, on the black bough of a snow flecked maple,
Fearless and gay as our love,
A bluejay cocked his crest!
Oh who can tell the range of joy
Or set the bounds of beauty?

In a Restaurant

The darkened street was muffled with the snow,
 The falling flakes had made your shoulders white,
 And when we found a shelter from the night
Its glamor fell upon us like a blow.
The clash of dishes and the viol and bow
 Mingled beneath the fever of the light.
 The heat was full of savors, and the bright
Laughter of women lured the wine to flow.
A little child ate nothing while she sat
 Watching a woman at a table there
Lean to a kiss beneath a drooping hat.
  The hour went by, we rose and turned to go,
 The somber street received us from the glare,
  And once more on your shoulders fell the snow.

JOY

I am wild, I will sing to the trees,
  I will sing to the stars in the sky,
I love, I am loved, he is mine,
  Now at last I can die!

I am sandaled with wind and with flame,
  I have heart-fire and singing to give,
I can tread on the grass or the stars,
  Now at last I can live!

In a Railroad Station

We stood in the shrill electric light,
    Dumb and sick in the whirling din
We who had all of love to say
    And a single second to say it in.

"Good-bye!" "Good-bye!"—you turned to go,
    I felt the train's slow heavy start,
You thought to see me cry, but oh
    My tears were hidden in my heart.

In the Train

Fields beneath a quilt of snow
    From which the rocks and stubble peep,
And in the west a shy white star
    That shivers as it wakes from sleep.

The restless rumble of the train,
    The drowsy people in the car,
Steel blue twilight in the world,
    And in my heart a timid star.

To One Away

I heard a cry in the night,
    A thousand miles it came,
Sharp as a flash of light,
    My name, my name!

It was your voice I heard,
    You waked and loved me so—
I send you back this word,
    I know, I know!

Song

Love me with your whole heart
    Or give no love to me,
Half-love is a poor thing,
    Neither bond nor free.

You must love me gladly
    Soul and body too,
Or else find a new love,
    And good-bye to you.

Deep in the Night

Deep in the night the cry of a swallow,
 Under the stars he flew,
Keen as pain was his call to follow
 Over the world to you.

Love in my heart is a cry forever
 Lost as the swallow's flight,
Seeking for you and never, never
 Stilled by the stars at night.

The India Wharf

Here in the velvet stillness
The wide sown fields fall to the faint horizon,
Sleeping in starlight. . .

A year ago we walked in the jangling city
Together. . . forgetful.
One by one we crossed the avenues,
Rivers of light, roaring in tumult,
And came to the narrow, knotted streets.
Thru the tense crowd
We went aloof, ecstatic, walking in wonder,
Unconscious of our motion.
Forever the foreign people with dark, deep-seeing eyes
Passed us and passed.
Lights and foreign words and foreign faces,
I forgot them all;
I only felt alive, defiant of all death and sorrow,
Sure and elated.

That was the gift you gave me. . .

The streets grew still more tangled,
And led at last to water black and glossy,
Flecked here and there with lights, faint and far off.
There on a shabby building was a sign
"The India Wharf" . . . and we turned back.

I always felt we could have taken ship
And crossed the bright green seas
To dreaming cities set on sacred streams
And palaces
Of ivory and scarlet.

I Shall not Care

When I am dead and over me bright April
    Shakes out her rain-drenched hair,
Tho' you should lean above me broken-hearted,
    I shall not care.

I shall have peace, as leafy trees are peaceful
    When rain bends down the bough,
And I shall be more silent and cold-hearted
    Than you are now.

Desert Pools

I love too much; I am a river
    Surging with spring that seeks the sea,
I am too generous a giver,
    Love will not stoop to drink of me.

His feet will turn to desert places
    Shadowless, reft of rain and dew,
Where stars stare down with sharpened faces
    From heavens pitilessly blue.

And there at midnight sick with faring,
    He will stoop down in his desire
To slake the thirst grown past all bearing
    In stagnant water keen as fire.

LONGING

I am not sorry for my soul
    That it must go unsatisfied,
For it can live a thousand times,
    Eternity is deep and wide.

I am not sorry for my soul,
    But oh, my body that must go
Back to a little drift of dust
    Without the joy it longed to know.

PITY

They never saw my lover's face,
    They only know our love was brief,
Wearing awhile a windy grace
    And passing like an autumn leaf.

They wonder why I do not weep,
    They think it strange that I can sing,
They say, "Her love was scarcely deep
    Since it has left so slight a sting."

They never saw my love, nor knew
    That in my heart's most secret place
I pity them as angels do
    Men who have never seen God's face.

After Parting

Oh I have sown my love so wide
    That he will find it everywhere;
It will awake him in the night,
    It will enfold him in the air.

I set my shadow in his sight
    And I have winged it with desire,
That it may be a cloud by day
    And in the night a shaft of fire.

Enough

It is enough for me by day
  To walk the same bright earth with him;
Enough that over us by night
  The same great roof of stars is dim.

I have no care to bind the wind
  Or set a fetter on the sea—
It is enough to feel his love
  Blow by like music over me.

ALCHEMY

I lift my heart as spring lifts up
    A yellow daisy to the rain;
My heart will be a lovely cup
    Altho' it holds but pain.

For I shall learn from flower and leaf
    That color every drop they hold,
To change the lifeless wine of grief
    To living gold.

FEBRUARY

They spoke of him I love
    With cruel words and gay;
My lips kept silent guard
    On all I could not say.

I heard, and down the street
    The lonely trees in the square
Stood in the winter wind
    Patient and bare.

I heard. . . oh voiceless trees
    Under the wind, I knew
The eager terrible spring
    Hidden in you.

Morning

I went out on an April morning
    All alone, for my heart was high,
I was a child of the shining meadow,
    I was a sister of the sky.

There in the windy flood of morning
    Longing lifted its weight from me,
Lost as a sob in the midst of cheering,
    Swept as a sea-bird out to sea.

MAY NIGHT

The spring is fresh and fearless
    And every leaf is new,
The world is brimmed with moonlight,
    The lilac brimmed with dew.

Here in the moving shadows
    I catch my breath and sing—
My heart is fresh and fearless
    And over-brimmed with spring.

Dusk in June

Evening, and all the birds
    In a chorus of shimmering sound
Are easing their hearts of joy
    For miles around.

The air is blue and sweet,
    The few first stars are white,—
Oh let me like the birds
    Sing before night.

LOVE-FREE

I am free of love as a bird flying south in the autumn,
Swift and intent, asking no joy from another,
Glad to forget all of the passion of April
    Ere it was love-free.

I am free of love, and I listen to music lightly,
But if he returned, if he should look at me deeply,
I should awake, I should awake and remember
    I am my lover's.

Summer Night, Riverside

In the wild soft summer darkness
How many and many a night we two together
Sat in the park and watched the Hudson
Wearing her lights like golden spangles
Glinting on black satin.
The rail along the curving pathway
Was low in a happy place to let us cross,
And down the hill a tree that dripped with bloom
Sheltered us
While your kisses and the flowers,
Falling, falling,
Tangled my hair. . .

The frail white stars moved slowly over the sky.

And now, far off
In the fragrant darkness
The tree is tremulous again with bloom
For June comes back.

Tonight what girl
When she goes home,
Dreamily before her mirror shakes from her hair
This year's blossoms, clinging in its coils ?

In a Subway Station

After a year I came again to the place;
The tireless lights and the reverberation,
The angry thunder of trains that burrow the ground,
The hunted, hurrying people were still the same—
But oh, another man beside me and not you!
Another voice and other eyes in mine!
And suddenly I turned and saw again
The gleaming curve of tracks, the bridge above—
They were burned deep into my heart before,
The night I watched them to avoid your eyes,
When you were saying, "Oh, look up at me!"
When you were saying, "Will you never love me?"
And when I answered with a lie. Oh then
You dropped your eyes. I felt your utter pain.
I would have died to say the truth to you.
After a year I came again to the place—
The hunted hurrying people were still the same. . .

SARA TEASDALE

After Love

There is no magic when we meet,
    We speak as other people do,
You work no miracle for me
    Nor I for you.

You were the wind and I the sea—
    There is no splendor any more,
I have grown listless as the pool
    Beside the shore.

But tho' the pool is safe from storm
    And from the tide has found surcease,
It grows more bitter than the sea,
    For all its peace.

Dooryard Roses

I have come the selfsame path
    To the selfsame door,
Years have left the roses there
    Burning as before.

While I watch them in the wind
    Quick the hot tears start—
Strange so frail a flame outlasts
    Fire in the heart.

A Prayer

Until I lose my soul and lie
    Blind to the beauty of the earth,
Deaf tho' a lyric wind goes by,
    Dumb in a storm of mirth;

Until my heart is quenched at length
    And I have left the land of men,
Oh let me love with all my strength
    Careless if I am loved again.

PART II

Indian Summer

Lyric night of the lingering Indian Summer,
Shadowy fields that are scentless but full of singing,
Never a bird, but the passionless chant of insects,
      Ceaseless, insistent.

The grasshopper's horn, and far off, high in the maples
The wheel of a locust leisurely grinding the silence,
Under a moon waning and worn and broken,
      Tired with summer.

Let me remember you, voices of little insects,
Weeds in the moonlight, fields that are tangled with asters,
Let me remember you, soon will the winter be on us,
      Snow-hushed and heartless.

Over my soul murmur your mute benediction
While I gaze, oh fields that rest after harvest,
As those who part look long in the eyes they lean to,
      Lest they forget them.

The Sea Wind

I am a pool in a peaceful place,
I greet the great sky face to face,
I know the stars and the stately moon
And the wind that runs with rippling shoon—
But why does it always bring to me
The far-off, beautiful sound of the sea?

The marsh-grass weaves me a wall of green,
But the wind comes whispering in between,
In the dead of night when the sky is deep
The wind comes waking me out of sleep—
Why does it always bring to me
The far-off, terrible call of the sea?

The Cloud

I am a cloud in the heaven's height,
The stars are lit for my delight,
Tireless and changeful, swift and free,
I cast my shadow on hill and sea—
But why do the pines on the mountain's crest
Call to me always, "Rest, rest"?

I throw my mantle over the moon
And I blind the sun on his throne at noon,
Nothing can tame me, nothing can bind,
I am a child of the heartless wind—
But oh the pines on the mountain's crest
Whispering always, "Rest, rest."

THE POOR HOUSE

Hope went by and Peace went by
    And would not enter in;
Youth went by and Health went by
    And Love that is their kin.

Those within the house shed tears
    On their bitter bread;
Some were old and some were mad,
    And some were sick a-bed.

Gray Death saw the wretched house
    And even he passed by—
"They have never lived," he said,
    "They can wait to die."

New Year's Dawn—Broadway

When the horns wear thin
And the noise, like a garment outworn,
Falls from the night,
The tattered and shivering night,
That thinks she is gay;
When the patient silence comes back,
And retires,
And returns,
Rebuffed by a ribald song,
Wounded by vehement cries,
Fleeing again to the stars—
Ashamed of her sister the night;
Oh, then they steal home,
The blinded, the pitiful ones
With their gew-gaws still in their hands,
Reeling with odorous breath
And thick, coarse words on their tongues.
They get them to bed, somehow,
And sleep the forgiving,
Comes thru the scattering tumult
And closes their eyes.
The stars sink down ashamed
And the dawn awakes,
Like a youth who steals from a brothel,
Dizzy and sick.

The Star

A white star born in the evening glow
Looked to the round green world below,
And saw a pool in a wooded place
That held like a jewel her mirrored face.
She said to the pool: "Oh, wondrous deep,
I love you, I give you my light to keep.
Oh, more profound than the moving sea
That never has shown myself to me!
Oh, fathomless as the sky is far,
Hold forever your tremulous star!"

But out of the woods as night grew cool
A brown pig came to the little pool;
It grunted and splashed and waded in
And the deepest place but reached its chin.
The water gurgled with tender glee
And the mud churned up in it turbidly.

The star grew pale and hid her face
In a bit of floating cloud like lace.

Doctors

Every night I lie awake
    And every day I lie abed
And hear the doctors, Pain and Death,
    Conferring at my head.

They speak in scientific tones,
    Professional and low—
One argues for a speedy cure,
    The other, sure and slow.

To one so humble as myself
    It should be matter for some pride
To have such noted fellows here,
    Conferring at my side.

The Inn of Earth

I came to the crowded Inn of Earth,
    And called for a cup of wine,
But the Host went by with averted eye
    From a thirst as keen as mine.

Then I sat down with weariness
    And asked a bit of bread,
But the Host went by with averted eye
    And never a word he said.

While always from the outer night
    The waiting souls came in
With stifled cries of sharp surprise
    At all the light and din.

"Then give me a bed to sleep," I said,
    "For midnight comes apace"—
But the Host went by with averted eye
    And I never saw his face.

"Since there is neither food nor rest,
    I go where I fared before"—
But the Host went by with averted eye
    And barred the outer door.

In the Carpenter's Shop

Mary sat in the corner dreaming,
    Dim was the room and low,
While in the dusk, the saw went screaming
        To and fro.

Jesus and Joseph toiled together,
    Mary was watching them,
Thinking of kings in the wintry weather
        At Bethlehem.

Mary sat in the corner thinking,
    Jesus had grown a man;
One by one her hopes were sinking
        As the years ran.

Jesus and Joseph toiled together,
    Mary's thoughts were far—
Angels sang in the wintry weather
        Under a star.

Mary sat in the corner weeping,
    Bitter and hot her tears—
Little faith were the angels keeping
        All the years.

The Carpenter's Son

The summer dawn came over-soon,
The earth was like hot iron at noon
      In Nazareth;
There fell no rain to ease the heat,
And dusk drew on with tired feet
      And stifled breath.

The shop was low and hot and square,
And fresh-cut wood made sharp the air,
      While all day long
The saw went tearing thru the oak
That moaned as tho' the tree's heart broke
      Beneath its wrong.

The narrow street was full of cries,
Of bickering and snarling lies
      In many keys—
The tongues of Egypt and of Rome
And lands beyond the shifting foam
      Of windy seas.

Sometimes a ruler riding fast
Scattered the dark crowds as he passed,
      And drove them close
In doorways, drawing broken breath
Lest they be trampled to their death
      Where the dust rose.

There in the gathering night and noise
A group of Galilean boys
      Crowding to see
Gray Joseph toiling with his son,
Saw Jesus, when the task was done,
      Turn wearily.

He passed them by with hurried tread
Silently, nor raised his head,
      He who looked up
Drinking all beauty from his birth
Out of the heaven and the earth
      As from a cup.

And Mary, who was growing old,
Knew that the pottage would be cold
      When he returned;
He hungered only for the night,
And westward, bending sharp and bright,
      The thin moon burned.

He reached the open western gate
Where whining halt and leper wait,
      And came at last
To the blue desert, where the deep
Great seas of twilight lay asleep,
      Windless and vast.

With shining eyes the stars awoke,
The dew lay heavy on his cloak,
      The world was dim;
And in the stillness he could hear
His secret thoughts draw very near
      And call to him.

Faint voices lifted shrill with pain
And multitudinous as rain;
      From all the lands
And all the villages thereof
Men crying for the gift of love
      With outstretched hands.

Voices that called with ceaseless crying,
The broken and the blind, the dying,
      And those grown dumb

Beneath oppression, and he heard
Upon their lips a single word,
   "Come!"

Their cries engulfed him like the night,
The moon put out her placid light
   And black and low
Nearer the heavy thunder drew,
Hushing the voices. . . yet he knew
   That he would go.

A quick-spun thread of lightning burns,
And for a flash the day returns—
   He only hears
Joseph, an old man bent and white
Toiling alone from morn till night
   Thru all the years.

Swift clouds make all the heavens blind,
A storm is running on the wind—
   He only sees
How Mary will stretch out her hands
Sobbing, who never understands
   Voices like these.

The Mother of a Poet

She is too kind, I think, for mortal things,
Too gentle for the gusty ways of earth;
God gave to her a shy and silver mirth,
And made her soul as clear
And softly singing as an orchard spring's
In sheltered hollows all the sunny year—
A spring that thru the leaning grass looks up
And holds all heaven in its clarid cup,
Mirror to holy meadows high and blue
With stars like drops of dew.

I love to think that never tears at night
Have made her eyes less bright;
That all her girlhood thru
Never a cry of love made over-tense
Her voice's innocence;
That in her hands have lain,
Flowers beaten by the rain,
And little birds before they learned to sing
Drowned in the sudden ecstasy of spring.

I love to think that with a wistful wonder
She held her baby warm against her breast;
That never any fear awoke whereunder
She shuddered at her gift, or trembled lest
Thru the great doors of birth
Here to a windy earth
She lured from heaven a half-unwilling guest.

She caught and kept his first vague flickering smile,
The faint upleaping of his spirit's fire;
And for a long sweet while
In her was all he asked of earth or heaven—
But in the end how far,
Past every shaken star,
Should leap at last that arrow-like desire,

His full-grown manhood's keen
Ardor toward the unseen
Dark mystery beyond the Pleiads seven.
And in her heart she heard
His first dim-spoken word—
She only of them all could understand,
Flushing to feel at last
The silence over-past,
Thrilling as tho' her hand had touched God's hand.
But in the end how many words
Winged on a flight she could not follow,
Farther than skyward lark or swallow,
His lips should free to lands she never knew;
Braver than white sea-faring birds
With a fearless melody,
Flying over a shining sea,
A star-white song between the blue and blue.

Oh I have seen a lake as clear and fair
As it were molten air,
Lifting a lily upward to the sun.
How should the water know the glowing heart
That ever to the heaven lifts its fire,
A golden and unchangeable desire?
The water only knows
The faint and rosy glows
Of under-petals, opening apart.
Yet in the soul of earth,
Deep in the primal ground,
Its searching roots are wound,
And centuries have struggled toward its birth.
So, in the man who sings,
All of the voiceless horde
From the cold dawn of things
Have their reward;
All in whose pulses ran
Blood that is his at last,
From the first stooping man
Far in the winnowed past.

SARA TEASDALE

Out of the tumult of their love and mating
Each one created, seeing life was good—
Dumb, till at last the song that they were waiting
Breaks like brave April thru a wintry wood.
But what of her whose heart is troubled by it,
The mother who would soothe and set him free,
Fearing the song's storm-shaken ecstasy—
Oh, as the moon that has no power to quiet
The strong wind-driven sea.

In Memoriam F. O. S.

You go a long and lovely journey,
      For all the stars, like burning dew,
Are luminous and luring footprints
      Of souls adventurous as you.

Oh, if you lived on earth elated,
      How is it now that you can run
Free of the weight of flesh and faring
      Far past the birthplace of the sun?

Twilight

The stately tragedy of dusk
    Drew to its perfect close,
The virginal white evening star
    Sank, and the red moon rose.

Swallow Flight

I love my hour of wind and light,
    I love men's faces and their eyes,
I love my spirit's veering flight
    Like swallows under evening skies,

Thoughts

When I can make my thoughts come forth
    To walk like ladies up and down,
Each one puts on before the glass
    Her most becoming hat and gown.

But oh, the shy and eager thoughts
    That hide and will not get them dressed,
Why is it that they always seem
    So much more lovely than the rest?

To Dick, on his Sixth Birthday

Tho' I am very old and wise,
    And you are neither wise nor old,
When I look far into your eyes,
    I know things I was never told:
I know how flame must strain and fret
Prisoned in a mortal net;
How joy with over-eager wings,
Bruises the small heart where he sings;
How too much life, like too much gold,
Is sometimes very hard to hold. . .
All that is talking—I know
This much is true, six years ago
An angel living near the moon
Walked thru the sky and sang a tune
Plucking stars to make his crown—
And suddenly two stars fell down,
Two falling arrows made of light.
Six years ago this very night
I saw them fall and wondered why
The angel dropped them from the sky—
But when I saw your eyes I knew
The angel sent the stars to you.

To Rose

Rose, when I remember you,
Little lady, scarcely two,
I am suddenly aware
Of the angels in the air.
All your softly gracious ways
Make an island in my days
Where my thoughts fly back to be
Sheltered from too strong a sea.
All your luminous delight
Shines before me in the night
When I grope for sleep and find
Only shadows in my mind.

Rose, when I remember you,
White and glowing, pink and new,
With so swift a sense of fun
Altho' life has just begun;
With so sure a pride of place
In your very infant face,
I should like to make a prayer
To the angels in the air:
"If an angel ever brings
Me a baby in her wings,
Please be certain that it grows
Very, very much like Rose."

The Fountain

Oh in the deep blue night
    The fountain sang alone;
It sang to the drowsy heart
    Of the satyr carved in stone.

The fountain sang and sang
    But the satyr never stirred—
Only the great white moon
    In the empty heaven heard.

The fountain sang and sang
    And on the marble rim
The milk-white peacocks slept,
    Their dreams were strange and dim.

Bright dew was on the grass,
    And on the ilex dew,
The dreamy milk-white birds
    Were all a-glisten too.

The fountain sang and sang
    The things one cannot tell,
The dreaming peacocks stirred
    And the gleaming dew-drops fell.

THE ROSE

Beneath my chamber window
Pierrot was singing, singing;
    I heard his lute the whole night thru
        Until the east was red.
Alas, alas, Pierrot,
I had no rose for flinging
    Save one that drank my tears for dew
        Before its leaves were dead.

I found it in the darkness,
I kissed it once and threw it,
    The petals scattered over him,
        His song was turned to joy;
And he will never know—
Alas, the one who knew it!—
    The rose was plucked when dusk was dim
        Beside a laughing boy.

DREAMS

I gave my life to another lover,
    I gave my love, and all, and all—
But over a dream the past will hover,
    Out of a dream the past will call.

I tear myself from sleep with a shiver
    But on my breast a kiss is hot,
And by my bed the ghostly giver
    Is waiting tho' I see him not.

"I am Not Yours"

I am not yours, not lost in you,
    Not lost, altho' I long to be
Lost as a candle lit at noon,
    Lost as a snow-flake in the sea.

You love me, and I find you still
    A spirit beautiful and bright,
Yet I am I, who long to be
    Lost as a light is lost in light.

Oh plunge me deep in love—put out
    My senses, leave me deaf and blind,
Swept by the tempest of your love,
    A taper in a rushing wind.

PIERROT'S SONG

(For a picture by Dugald Walker)

Lady, light in the east hangs low,
    Draw your veils of dream apart,
Under the casement stands Pierrot
    Making a song to ease his heart.
(Yet do not break the song too soon—
    I love to sing in the paling moon.)

The petals are falling, heavy with dew,
    The stars have fainted out of the sky,
Come to me, come, or else I too,
    Faint with the weight of love will die.
(She comes—alas, I hoped to make
    Another stanza for her sake!)

NIGHT IN ARIZONA

The moon is a charring ember
    Dying into the dark;
Off in the crouching mountains
        Coyotes bark.

The stars are heavy in heaven,
    Too great for the sky to hold—
What if they fell and shattered
        The earth with gold?

No lights are over the mesa,
    The wind is hard and wild,
I stand at the darkened window
        And cry like a child.

Dusk in War Time

A half-hour more and you will lean
  To gather me close in the old sweet way—
But oh, to the woman over the sea
  Who will come at the close of day?

A half-hour more and I will hear
  The key in the latch and the strong quick tread—
But oh, the woman over the sea
  Waiting at dusk for one who is dead!

Spring in War Time

I feel the Spring far off, far off,
    The faint far scent of bud and leaf—
Oh how can Spring take heart to come
    To a world in grief,
        Deep grief?

The sun turns north, the days grow long,
    Later the evening star grows bright—
How can the daylight linger on
    For men to fight,
        Still fight?

The grass is waking in the ground,
    Soon it will rise and blow in waves—
How can it have the heart to sway
    Over the graves,
        New graves?

Under the boughs where lovers walked
    The apple-blooms will shed their breath—
But what of all the lovers now
    Parted by death,
        Gray Death?

WHILE I MAY

Wind and hail and veering rain,
    Driven mist that veils the day,
Soul's distress and body's pain,
    I would bear you while I may.

I would love you if I might,
    For so soon my life will be
Buried in a lasting night,
    Even pain denied to me.

Debt

What do I owe to you
    Who loved me deep and long?
You never gave my spirit wings
    Or gave my heart a song.

But oh, to him I loved
    Who loved me not at all,
I owe the little open gate
    That led thru heaven's wall.

From the North

The northern woods are delicately sweet,
　　The lake is folded softly by the shore,
　　But I am restless for the subway's roar,
The thunder and the hurrying of feet.
I try to sleep, but still my eyelids beat
　　Against the image of the tower that bore
　　Me high aloft, as if thru heaven's door
I watched the world from God's unshaken seat.
I would go back and breathe with quickened sense
　　The tunnel's strong hot breath of powdered steel;
But at the ferries I should leave the tense
　　　　Dark air behind, and I should mount and be
　　One among many who are thrilled to feel
　　　　The first keen sea-breath from the open sea.

The Lights of New York

The lightning spun your garment for the night
    Of silver filaments with fire shot thru,
    A broidery of lamps that lit for you
The steadfast splendor of enduring light.
The moon drifts dimly in the heaven's height,
    Watching with wonder how the earth she knew
    That lay so long wrapped deep in dark and dew,
Should wear upon her breast a star so white.
The festivals of Babylon were dark
    With flaring flambeaux that the wind blew down;
The Saturnalia were a wild boy's lark
    With rain-quenched torches dripping thru the town—
But you have found a god and filched from him
A fire that neither wind nor rain can dim.

Sea Longing

A thousand miles beyond this sun-steeped wall
    Somewhere the waves creep cool along the sand,
    The ebbing tide forsakes the listless land
With the old murmur, long and musical;
The windy waves mount up and curve and fall,
    And round the rocks the foam blows up like snow,—
    Tho' I am inland far, I hear and know,
For I was born the sea's eternal thrall.
I would that I were there and over me
    The cold insistence of the tide would roll,
    Quenching this burning thing men call the soul,—
Then with the ebbing I should drift and be
    Less than the smallest shell along the shoal,
Less than the sea-gulls calling to the sea.

THE RIVER

I came from the sunny valleys
    And sought for the open sea,
For I thought in its gray expanses
    My peace would come to me.

I came at last to the ocean
    And found it wild and black,
And I cried to the windless valleys,
    "Be kind and take me back!"

But the thirsty tide ran inland,
    And the salt waves drank of me,
And I who was fresh as the rainfall
    Am bitter as the sea.

Leaves

One by one, like leaves from a tree,
All my faiths have forsaken me;
But the stars above my head
Burn in white and delicate red,
And beneath my feet the earth
Brings the sturdy grass to birth.
I who was content to be
But a silken-singing tree,
But a rustle of delight
In the wistful heart of night—
I have lost the leaves that knew
Touch of rain and weight of dew.
Blinded by a leafy crown
I looked neither up nor down—
But the little leaves that die
Have left me room to see the sky;
Now for the first time I know
Stars above and earth below.

The Answer

When I go back to earth
And all my joyous body
Puts off the red and white
That once had been so proud,
If men should pass above
With false and feeble pity,
My dust will find a voice
To answer them aloud:

"Be still, I am content,
Take back your poor compassion,
Joy was a flame in me
Too steady to destroy;
Lithe as a bending reed
Loving the storm that sways her—
I found more joy in sorrow
Than you could find in joy."

PART III

OVER THE ROOFS

I

Oh chimes set high on the sunny tower
    Ring on, ring on unendingly,
Make all the hours a single hour,
For when the dusk begins to flower,
    The man I love will come to me! . . .

But no, go slowly as you will,
    I should not bid you hasten so,
For while I wait for love to come,
Some other girl is standing dumb,
    Fearing her love will go.

II

Oh white steam over the roofs, blow high!
    Oh chimes in the tower ring clear and free !
Oh sun awake in the covered sky,
    For the man I love, loves me I. . .

Oh drifting steam disperse and die,
    Oh tower stand shrouded toward the south,—
Fate heard afar my happy cry,
    And laid her finger on my mouth.

III

The dusk was blue with blowing mist,
    The lights were spangles in a veil,
And from the clamor far below
    Floated faint music like a wail.

It voiced what I shall never speak,
    My heart was breaking all night long,

But when the dawn was hard and gray,
    My tears distilled into a song.

IV

I said, "I have shut my heart
    As one shuts an open door,
That Love may starve therein
    And trouble me no more."

But over the roofs there came
    The wet new wind of May,
And a tune blew up from the curb
    Where the street-pianos play.

My room was white with the sun
    And Love cried out in me,
"I am strong, I will break your heart
    Unless you set me free."

A Cry

Oh, there are eyes that he can see,
    And hands to make his hands rejoice,
But to my lover I must be
        Only a voice.

Oh, there are breasts to bear his head,
    And lips whereon his lips can lie,
But I must be till I am dead
        Only a cry.

CHANCE

How many times we must have met
    Here on the street as strangers do,
Children of chance we were, who passed
    The door of heaven and never knew.

Immortal

So soon my body will have gone
    Beyond the sound and sight of men,
And tho' it wakes and suffers now,
    Its sleep will be unbroken then;
But oh, my frail immortal soul
    That will not sleep forevermore,
A leaf borne onward by the blast,
    A wave that never finds the shore.

AFTER DEATH

Now while my lips are living
    Their words must stay unsaid,
And will my soul remember
    To speak when I am dead?

Yet if my soul remembered
    You would not heed it, dear,
For now you must not listen,
    And then you could not hear.

TESTAMENT

I said, "I will take my life
    And throw it away;
I who was fire and song
    Will turn to clay."

"I will lie no more in the night
    With shaken breath,
I will toss my heart in the air
    To be caught by Death."

But out of the night I heard,
    Like the inland sound of the sea,
The hushed and terrible sob
    Of all humanity.

Then I said, "Oh who am I
    To scorn God to his face?
I will bow my head and stay
    And suffer with my race."

Gifts

I gave my first love laughter,
    I gave my second tears,
I gave my third love silence
    Thru all the years.

My first love gave me singing,
    My second eyes to see,
But oh, it was my third love
    Who gave my soul to me.

PART IV

From the Sea

All beauty calls you to me, and you seem,
Past twice a thousand miles of shifting sea,
To reach me. You are as the wind I breathe
Here on the ship's sun-smitten topmost deck,
With only light between the heavens and me.
I feel your spirit and I close my eyes,
Knowing the bright hair blowing in the sun,
The eager whisper and the searching eyes.

Listen, I love you. Do not turn your face
Nor touch me. Only stand and watch awhile
The blue unbroken circle of the sea.
Look far away and let me ease my heart
Of words that beat in it with broken wing.
Look far away, and if I say too much,
Forget that I am speaking. Only watch,
How like a gull that sparkling sinks to rest,
The foam-crest drifts along a happy wave
Toward the bright verge, the boundary of the world.

I am so weak a thing, praise me for this,
That in some strange way I was strong enough
To keep my love unuttered and to stand
Altho' I longed to kneel to you that night
You looked at me with ever-calling eyes.
Was I not calm? And if you guessed my love
You thought it something delicate and free,
Soft as the sound of fir-trees in the wind,
Fleeting as phosphorescent stars in foam.
Yet in my heart there was a beating storm
Bending my thoughts before it, and I strove
To say too little lest I say too much,
And from my eyes to drive love's happy shame.
Yet when I heard your name the first far time
It seemed like other names to me, and I
Was all unconscious, as a dreaming river

That nears at last its long predestined sea;
And when you spoke to me, I did not know
That to my life's high altar came its priest.
But now I know between my God and me
You stand forever, nearer God than I,
And in your hands with faith and utter joy
I would that I could lay my woman's soul.

Oh, my love
To whom I cannot come with any gift
Of body or of soul, I pass and go.
But sometimes when you hear blown back to you
My wistful, far-off singing touched with tears,
Know that I sang for you alone to hear,
And that I wondered if the wind would bring
To him who tuned my heart its distant song.
So might a woman who in loneliness
Had borne a child, dreaming of days to come,
Wonder if it would please its father's eyes.
But long before I ever heard your name,
Always the undertone's unchanging note
In all my singing had prefigured you,
Foretold you as a spark foretells a flame.
Yet I was free as an untethered cloud
In the great space between the sky and sea,
And might have blown before the wind of joy
Like a bright banner woven by the sun.
I did not know the longing in the night—
You who have waked me cannot give me sleep.
All things in all the world can rest, but I,
Even the smooth brief respite of a wave
When it gives up its broken crown of foam,
Even that little rest I may not have.
And yet all quiet loves of friends, all joy
In all the piercing beauty of the world
I would give up—go blind forevermore,
Rather than have God blot from out my soul
Remembrance of your voice that said my name.

SARA TEASDALE

For us no starlight stilled the April fields,
No birds awoke in darkling trees for us,
Yet where we walked the city's street that night
Felt in our feet the singing fire of spring,
And in our path we left a trail of light
Soft as the phosphorescence of the sea
When night submerges in the vessel's wake
A heaven of unborn evanescent stars.

Vignettes Overseas

I

Off Gibraltar

Beyond the sleepy hills of Spain,
    The sun goes down in yellow mist,
The sky is fresh with dewy stars
    Above a sea of amethyst.

Yet in the city of my love
    High noon burns all the heavens bare—
For him the happiness of light,
    For me a delicate despair.

II

Off Algiers

Oh give me neither love nor tears,
    Nor dreams that sear the night with fire,
Go lightly on your pilgrimage
    Unburdened by desire.

Forget me for a month, a year,
    But, oh, beloved, think of me
When unexpected beauty burns
    Like sudden sunlight on the sea.

III

Naples

Nisida and Prosida are laughing in the light,
Capri is a dewy flower lifting into sight,
Posilipo kneels and looks in the burnished sea,
Naples crowds her million roofs close as close can be;

Round about the mountain's crest a flag of smoke is hung—
Oh when God made Italy he was gay and young!

IV

Capri

When beauty grows too great to bear
    How shall I ease me of its ache,
For beauty more than bitterness
    Makes the heart break.

Now while I watch the dreaming sea
    With isles like flowers against her breast,
Only one voice in all the world
    Could give me rest.

V

Night Song at Amalfi

I asked the heaven of stars
    What I should give my love—
It answered me with silence,
    Silence above.

I asked the darkened sea
    Down where the fishers go—
It answered me with silence,
    Silence below.

Oh, I could give him weeping,
    Or I could give him song—
But how can I give silence
    My whole life long?

VI

Ruins of Paestum

On lowlands where the temples lie
    The marsh-grass mingles with the flowers,
Only the little songs of birds
    Link the unbroken hours.

So in the end, above my heart
    Once like the city wild and gay,
The slow white stars will pass by night,
    The swift brown birds by day.

VII

Rome

Oh for the rising moon
    Over the roofs of Rome,
And swallows in the dusk
    Circling a darkened dome!

Oh for the measured dawns
    That pass with folded wings—
How can I let them go
    With unremembered things?

VIII

Florence

The bells ring over the Anno,
    Midnight, the long, long chime;
Here in the quivering darkness
    I am afraid of time.

Oh, gray bells cease your tolling,
    Time takes too much from me,

And yet to rock and river
    He gives eternity.

IX

Villa Serbelloni, Bellaggio

The fountain shivers lightly in the rain,
    The laurels drip, the fading roses fall,
The marble satyr plays a mournful strain
    That leaves the rainy fragrance musical.

Oh dripping laurel, Phoebus sacred tree,
    Would that swift Daphne's lot might come to me,
Then would I still my soul and for an hour
    Change to a laurel in the glancing shower.

X

Stresa

The moon grows out of the hills
    A yellow flower,
The lake is a dreamy bride
    Who waits her hour.

Beauty has filled my heart,
    It can hold no more,
It is full, as the lake is full,
    From shore to shore.

XI

Hamburg

The day that I come home,
    What will you find to say,—
Words as light as foam
    With laughter light as spray?

Yet say what words you will
    The day that I come home;
I shall hear the whole deep ocean
    Beating under the foam.

PART V

Sappho

I

Midnight, and in the darkness not a sound,
So, with hushed breathing, sleeps the autumn night;
Only the white immortal stars shall know,
Here in the house with the low-lintelled door,
How, for the last time, I have lit the lamp.
I think you are not wholly careless now,
Walls that have sheltered me so many an hour,
Bed that has brought me ecstasy and sleep,
Floors that have borne me when a gale of joy
Lifted my soul and made me half a god.
Farewell! Across the threshold many feet
Shall pass, but never Sappho's feet again.
Girls shall come in whom love has made aware
Of all their swaying beauty—they shall sing,
But never Sappho's voice, like golden fire,
Shall seek for heaven thru your echoing rafters.
There shall be swallows bringing back the spring
Over the long blue meadows of the sea,
And south-wind playing on the reeds of rain,
But never Sappho's whisper in the night,
Never her love-cry when the lover comes.
Farewell! I close the door and make it fast.

The little street lies meek beneath the moon,
Running, as rivers run, to meet the sea.
I too go seaward and shall not return.
Oh garlands on the doorposts that I pass,
Woven of asters and of autumn leaves,
I make a prayer for you: Cypris be kind,
That every lover may be given love.
I shall not hasten lest the paving stones
Should echo with my sandals and awake
Those who are warm beneath the cloak of sleep,
Lest they should rise and see me and should say,

"Whither goes Sappho lonely in the night?"
Whither goes Sappho? Whither all men go,
But they go driven, straining back with fear,
And Sappho goes as lightly as a leaf
Blown from brown autumn forests to the sea.

Here on the rock Zeus lifted from the waves,
I shall await the waking of the dawn,
Lying beneath the weight of dark as one
Lies breathless, till the lover shall awake.
And with the sun the sea shall cover me—
I shall be less than the dissolving foam
Murmuring and melting on the ebbing tide;
I shall be less than spindrift, less than shells;
And yet I shall be greater than the gods,
For destiny no more can bow my soul
As rain bows down the watch-fires on the hills.
Yes, if my soul escape it shall aspire
To the white heaven as flame that has its will.
I go not bitterly, not dumb with pain,
Not broken by the ache of love—I go
As one grown tired lies down and hopes to sleep.
Yet they shall say: "It was for Cercolas;
She died because she could not bear her love."
They shall remember how we used to walk
Here on the cliff beneath the oleanders
In the long limpid twilight of the spring,
Looking toward Lemnos, where the amber sky
Was pierced with the faint arrow of a star.
How should they know the wind of a new beauty
Sweeping my soul had winnowed it with song?
I have been glad tho' love should come or go,
Happy as trees that find a wind to sway them,
Happy again when it has left them rest.
Others shall say, "Grave Dica wrought her death.
She would not lift her lips to take a kiss,
Or ever lift her eyes to take a smile.
She was a pool the winter paves with ice
That the wild hunter in the hills must leave

With thirst unslaked in the brief southward sun."
Ah Dica, it is not for thee I go;
And not for Phaon, tho' his ship lifts sail
Here in the windless harbor for the south.
Oh, darkling deities that guard the Nile,
Watch over one whose gods are far away.
Egypt, be kind to him, his eyes are deep—
Yet they are wrong who say it was for him.
How should they know that Sappho lived and died
Faithful to love, not faithful to the lover,
Never transfused and lost in what she loved,
Never so wholly loving nor at peace.
I asked for something greater than I found,
And every time that love has made me weep,
I have rejoiced that love could be so strong;
For I have stood apart and watched my soul
Caught in the gust of passion, as a bird
With baffled wings against the dusty whirlwind
Struggles and frees itself to find the sky.
It is not for a single god I go;
I have grown weary of the winds of heaven.
I will not be a reed to hold the sound
Of whatsoever breath the gods may blow,
Turning my torment into music for them.
They gave me life; the gift was bountiful,
I lived with the swift singing strength of fire,
Seeking for beauty as a flame for fuel—
Beauty in all things and in every hour.
The gods have given life—I gave them song;
The debt is paid and now I turn to go.
The breath of dawn blows the stars out like lamps,
There is a rim of silver on the sea,
As one grown tired who hopes to sleep, I go.

II

Oh Litis, little slave, why will you sleep?
These long Egyptian noons bend down your head
Bowed like the yarrow with a yellow bee.

There, lift your eyes no man has ever kindled,
Dark eyes that wait like faggots for the fire.
See how the temple's solid square of shade
Points north to Lesbos, and the splendid sea
That you have never seen, oh evening-eyed.
Yet have you never wondered what the Nile
Is seeking always, restless and wild with spring
And no less in the winter, seeking still?
How shall I tell you? Can you think of fields
Greater than Gods could till, more blue than night
Sown over with the stars; and delicate
With filmy nets of foam that come and go?
It is more cruel and more compassionate
Than harried earth. It takes with unconcern
And quick forgetting, rapture of the rain
And agony of thunder, the moon's white
Soft-garmented virginity, and then
The insatiable ardor of the sun.
And me it took. But there is one more strong,
Love, that came laughing from the elder seas,
The Cyprian, the mother of the world;
She gave me love who only asked for death—
I who had seen much sorrow in men's eyes
And in my own too sorrowful a fire.
I was a sister of the stars, and yet
Shaken with pain; sister of birds and yet
The wings that bore my soul were very tired.
I watched the careless spring too many times
Light her green torches in a hungry wind;
Too many times I watched them flare, and then
Fall to forsaken embers in the autumn.
And I was sick of all things—even song.
In the dull autumn dawn I turned to death,
Buried my living body in the sea,
The strong cold sea that takes and does not give—
But there is one more strong, the Cyprian.
Litis, to wake from sleep and find your eyes
Met in their first fresh upward gaze by love,
Filled with love's happy shame from other eyes,

Dazzled with tenderness and drowned in light
As tho' you looked unthinking at the sun,
Oh Litis, that is joy! But if you came
Not from the sunny shallow pool of sleep,
But from the sea of death, the strangling sea
Of night and nothingness, and waked to find
Love looking down upon you, glad and still,
Strange and yet known forever, that is peace.
So did he lean above me. Not a word
He spoke; I only heard the morning sea
Singing against his happy ship, the keen
And straining joy of wind-awakened sails
And songs of mariners, and in myself
The precious pain of arms that held me fast.
They warmed the cold sea out of all my blood;
I slept, feeling his eyes above my sleep.
There on the ship with wines and olives laden,
Led by the stars to far invisible ports,
Egypt and islands of the inner seas,
Love came to me, and Cercolas was love.

III

The twilight's inner flame grows blue and deep,
And in my Lesbos, over leagues of sea,
The temples glimmer moon-wise in the trees.
Twilight has veiled the little flower-face
Here on my heart, but still the night is kind
And leaves her warm sweet weight against my breast.
Am I that Sappho who would run at dusk
Along the surges creeping up the shore
When tides came in to ease the hungry beach,
And running, running till the night was black,
Would fall forespent upon the chilly sand
And quiver with the winds from off the sea?
Ah quietly the shingle waits the tides
Whose waves are stinging kisses, but to me
Love brought no peace, nor darkness any rest.
I crept and touched the foam with fevered hands

And cried to Love, from whom the sea is sweet,
From whom the sea is bitterer than death.
Ah, Aphrodite, if I sing no more
To thee, God's daughter, powerful as God,
It is that thou hast made my life too sweet
To hold the added sweetness of a song.
There is a quiet at the heart of love,
And I have pierced the pain and come to peace
I hold my peace, my Cleïs, on my heart;
And softer than a little wild bird's wing
Are kisses that she pours upon my mouth.
Ah never any more when spring like fire
Will flicker in the newly opened leaves,
Shall I steal forth to seek for solitude
Beyond the lure of light Alcaeus' lyre,
Beyond the sob that stilled Erinna's voice.
Ah, never with a throat that aches with song,
Beneath the white uncaring sky of spring,
Shall I go forth to hide awhile from Love
The quiver and the crying of my heart.
Still I remember how I strove to flee
The love-note of the birds, and bowed my head
To hurry faster, but upon the ground
I saw two wingèd shadows side by side,
And all the world's spring passion stifled me.
Ah, Love there is no fleeing from thy might,
No lonely place where thou hast never trod,
No desert thou hast left uncarpeted
With flowers that spring beneath thy perfect feet.
In many guises didst thou come to me;
I saw thee by the maidens while they danced,
Phaon allured me with a look of thine,
In Anactoria I knew thy grace,
I looked at Cercolas and saw thine eyes;
But never wholly, soul and body mine,
Didst thou bid any love me as I loved.
Now have I found the peace that fled from me;
Close, close against my heart I hold my world.

SARA TEASDALE

Ah, Love that made my life a Iyric cry,
Ah, Love that tuned my lips to Iyres of thine,
I taught the world thy music, now alone
I sing for one who falls asleep to hear.

A Note About the Author

Sara Teasdale (1884–1933) was an American poet. Born in St. Louis, Missouri, Teasdale suffered from poor health as a child before entering school at the age of ten. In 1904, after graduating from Hosmer Hall, Teasdale joined the group of female artists known as The Potters, who published *The Potter's Wheel*, a monthly literary and visual arts magazine, from 1904 to 1907. With her first two collections—*Sonnets to Duse and Other Poems* (1907) and *Helen of Troy and Other Poems* (1911)—Teasdale earned a reputation as a gifted lyric poet from critics and readers alike. In 1916, following the publication of her bestselling *Rivers to the Sea* (1915), she moved to New York City with her husband Ernst Filsinger. There, she won the 1918 Pulitzer Prize for *Love Songs* (1917), her fourth collection. Frustrated with Filsinger's prolonged absences while traveling for work, she divorced him in 1929 and moved to another apartment in the Upper West Side. Renewing her friendship with poet Vachel Lindsay, she continued to write and publish poems until her death by suicide in 1933.

A Note from the Publisher

Spanning many genres, from non-fiction essays to literature classics to children's books and lyric poetry, Mint Edition books showcase the master works of our time in a modern new package. The text is freshly typeset, is clean and easy to read, and features a new note about the author in each volume. Many books also include exclusive new introductory material. Every book boasts a striking new cover, which makes it as appropriate for collecting as it is for gift giving. Mint Edition books are only printed when a reader orders them, so natural resources are not wasted. We're proud that our books are never manufactured in excess and exist only in the exact quantity they need to be read and enjoyed.

bookfinity™

Discover more of your favorite classics with Bookfinity™.

- Track your reading with custom book lists.
- Get great book recommendations for your personalized Reader Type.
- Add reviews for your favorite books.
- AND MUCH MORE!

Visit **bookfinity.com** and take the fun Reader Type quiz to get started.

Enjoy our classic and modern companion pairings!

Classic & Modern

Printed in the USA
CPSIA information can be obtained
at www.ICGtesting.com
JSHW082356140824
68134JS00020B/2110

9 781513 295954